The Countries

Scotland

Tamara L. Britton

ABDO Publishing Company

visit us at
www.abdopub.com

Published by ABDO Publishing Company, 4940 Viking Drive, Edina, Minnesota 55435.

Printed in the United States.

Photo Credits: Corbis, AP/Wide World
Contributing Editors: Kristin Van Cleaf, Stephanie Hedlund
Art Direction & Maps: Neil Klinepier

Library of Congress Cataloging-in-Publication Data

Britton, Tamara L., 1963-
Scotland / Tamara L. Britton.
p. cm. -- (The countries)
Includes index.
Summary: An introduction to the history, geography, economy, government, people, and more of Scotland. Includes a recipe for the dish called skirlie.
ISBN 1-57765-843-4
1. Scotland--Juvenile literature. [1. Scotland.] I. Title. II. Series.

DA762 .B68 2002
941.1--dc21

2002020796

Contents

Sodan!

Hello from Scotland! Scotland is a country in the **United Kingdom**. It occupies the northern part of the island of Great Britain.

Scotland's rugged land is made up of Highlands and Lowlands. Most of the country's people live in rural areas in the Lowlands. Scotland's people are called Scots. They speak English and Scottish Gaelic (GAY-lik). Most practice the Presbyterian religion.

The United Kingdom governs Scotland. But in 1997, Scotland created its own **parliament**. Now, Scots have greater control over their own affairs. The new parliament met for the first time in 1999. Scotland's people and government are working together to make Scotland a great place to live.

Sodan ***from*** **Scotland!**

Fast Facts

OFFICIAL NAME: Scotland
CAPITAL: Edinburgh

LAND
- Area: 30,418 square miles (78,782 sq km)
- Mountain Ranges: Northwest Highlands, Grampian Mountains
- Highest Point: Ben Nevis 4,406 feet (1,343 m)
- Major Rivers: Clyde, Forth, Tay
- Major Lakes: Loch Lomond, Loch Ness

PEOPLE
- Population: 5,114,600 (2000 est.)
- Major Cities: Edinburgh, Glasgow, Aberdeen
- Languages: English, Scottish Gaelic
- Religion: Presbyterian (Church of Scotland)

GOVERNMENT
- Form: Constitutional monarchy
- Head of State: King or queen
- Head of Government: Prime minister
- Legislature: Two house parliament
- Flag: A white *X* on a blue field
- National Anthem: "Flower of Scotland"
- Nationhood: 1314

ECONOMY
- Agricultural Products: Wheat, barley, oats, sugar beets, rye, potatoes; cattle, sheep, pigs, dairy products
- Mining Products: Petroleum, limestone, peat, coal
- Manufactured Products: Electrical and optical equipment, food products, paper, textiles
- Money: Scottish pound sterling (1 pound = 100 pence)

Scotland's flag

Paper and coin versions of the Scottish pound

Timeline

A.D. 43	Romans invade Scotland
400s	Roman Empire collapses, Romans leave Scotland
500s	Celts establish a monarchy
1296	King Edward I of England invades Scotland; William Wallace leads rebellions against England
1320	Scots declare independence from England
1328	Robert the Bruce is recognized as king
1500s	Reformation sweeps through Europe
1603	King James VI becomes King James I of Great Britain
1707	Act of Union creates the United Kingdom of Great Britain
1997	Scotland creates a separate parliament
1999	Scottish Parliament meets for the first time

History

People have lived in Scotland for more than 7,000 years. In A.D. 43, the Romans invaded Scotland. They called Scotland's people Picts (PIKTS), because they painted designs on their faces. The Picts fought the Romans, but could not defeat them. The Romans left when their empire collapsed in the 400s.

In the 500s, Celts (KELTS) came from western Europe. They established a monarchy in Scotland, and called themselves Scots. In 843, Kenneth MacAlpin was king of the Scots. He became king of the Picts, too, and began the Kingdom of Alba.

Scottish and English kings fought each other for control of Scotland. During the reign (RAYN) of Alexander III, a border was established between England and Scotland. For a time, this slowed the fighting.

But England's King Edward I invaded and tried to rule Scotland in 1296. William Wallace led Scots to many victories in **rebellion** against the English. The Scots declared independence from England in 1320. In 1328, King Edward recognized Robert the Bruce as King Robert I of Scotland. During Robert's reign, Scotland kept close ties with France.

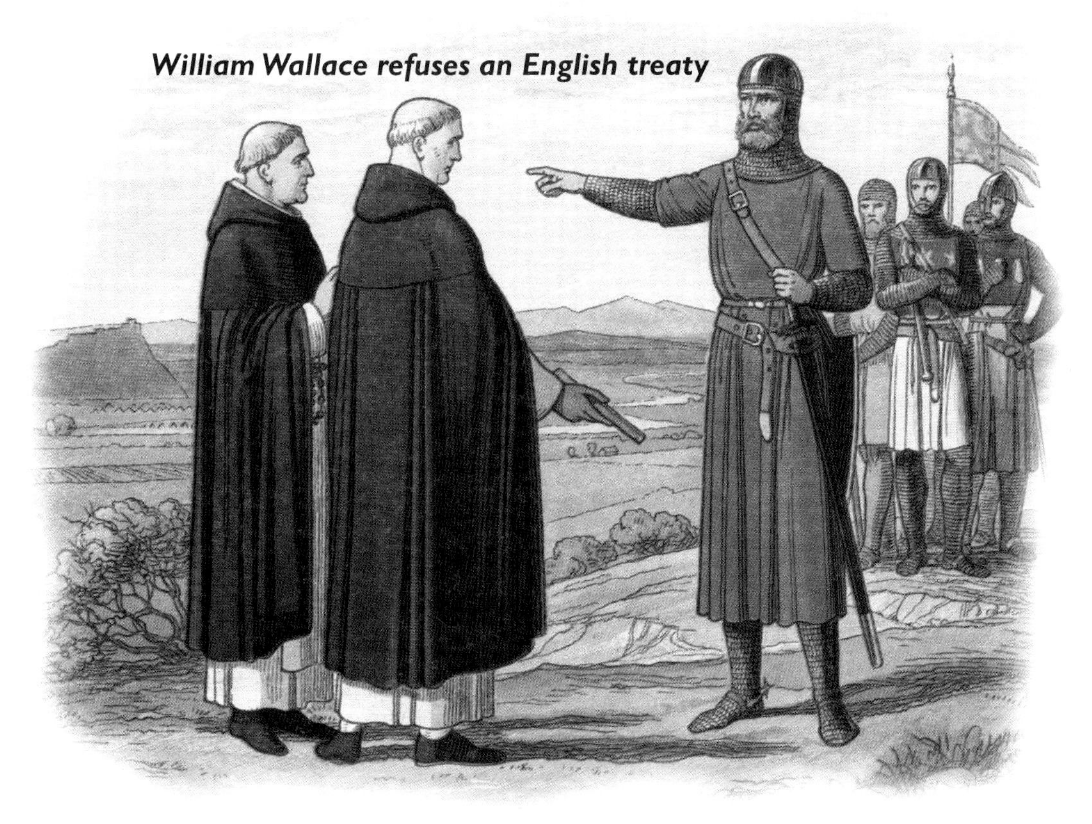

William Wallace refuses an English treaty

In the 1500s, there was widespread disagreement about the interpretation of the Christian faith. This started a movement called the **Reformation**. Many Protestant churches were created during this time. Catholics and Protestants fought violently over which church was best.

Mary, Queen of Scots, became Scotland's ruler in 1542. But she was only six days old. So she was sent to France and her mother ruled for her. Mary returned to rule Scotland in 1565. But she was forced to flee two years later. Her one-year-old son, James VI, then became king of Scotland.

Mary was Catholic, and England's Queen Elizabeth I was Protestant. Elizabeth felt Mary and her beliefs were a threat to the English throne. So she had Mary **executed** in 1587.

Mary, Queen of Scots

When Queen Elizabeth I died in 1603, Scotland's King James VI became the king of England, too. He was then called King James I of Great Britain.

In 1638, Scots signed the National **Covenant** to resist English control of Scottish religion. In 1642, a **civil war** began in England.

General Oliver Cromwell led forces against Great Britain's King Charles I. Cromwell united England, Ireland, and Scotland. Charles I was killed in 1649, and Cromwell became head of state. He died in 1658, and Charles II became king two years later. Charles II dissolved the union of England, Ireland, and Scotland.

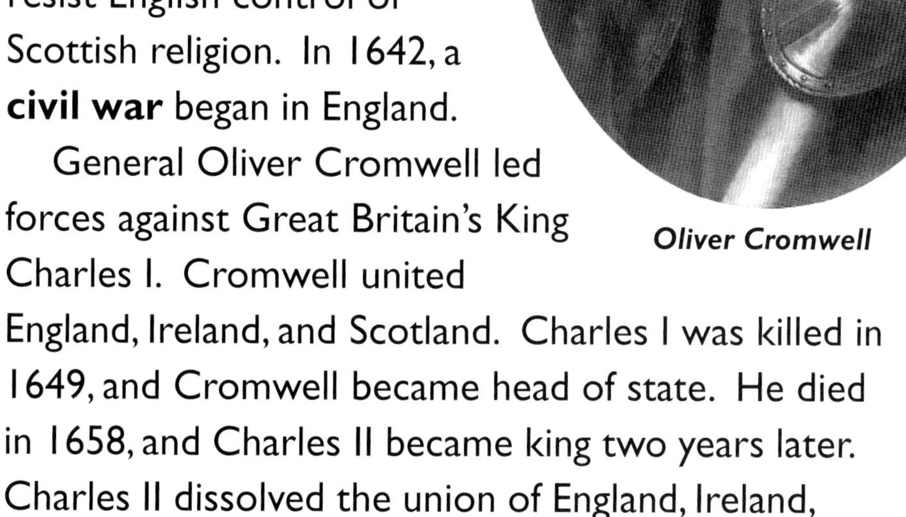

Oliver Cromwell

England and Scotland remained separate kingdoms under one monarch until the 1707 Act of Union. This agreement made England and Scotland into the **United Kingdom** of Great Britain.

Queen Anne was the last monarch from the Scottish House of Stuart. Then the English House of Hanover took the throne. The Scots **rebelled** in 1715 and 1745. Rebels tried to put a Scot back on the throne, but they were defeated both times.

In the 1800s, shipbuilding, mining, and iron and steel production caused Scotland's **economy** to grow. The country's population continued to increase. But the Scots continued to fight against England's rule.

In 1997, the Scots passed a **referendum** to create a **parliament** of their own. Scotland's parliament met for the first time in 1999.

Opposite page: Queen Elizabeth II of England attended the first meeting of the Scottish Parliament in 1999.

By 2000, Scotland's **economy** was based on tourism, electronics manufacturing, and **petroleum** fields in the North Sea. Today, Scotland's leaders continue to work toward independence.

The Land

Scotland takes up the northern third of the island of Great Britain. It is bordered by England on the south, the North Sea on the east, and the Atlantic Ocean on the other sides.

Scotland has a mild, maritime climate. This means temperatures are affected by the ocean. Winter occurs from October to May, and snow is common. Summer is cool, with temperatures ranging from 57 to 75°F (14 to 24°C).

The Highlands cover most of Scotland's land. The Southern Uplands and the Central Lowlands cover the rest. The Highlands has two major mountain ranges. They are the Northwest Highlands and the Grampian Mountains.

A series of *lochs* (LAHKS), or lakes, called Glen Mor separates the mountain ranges. Most of Scotland's *lochs* are in the Highland valleys.

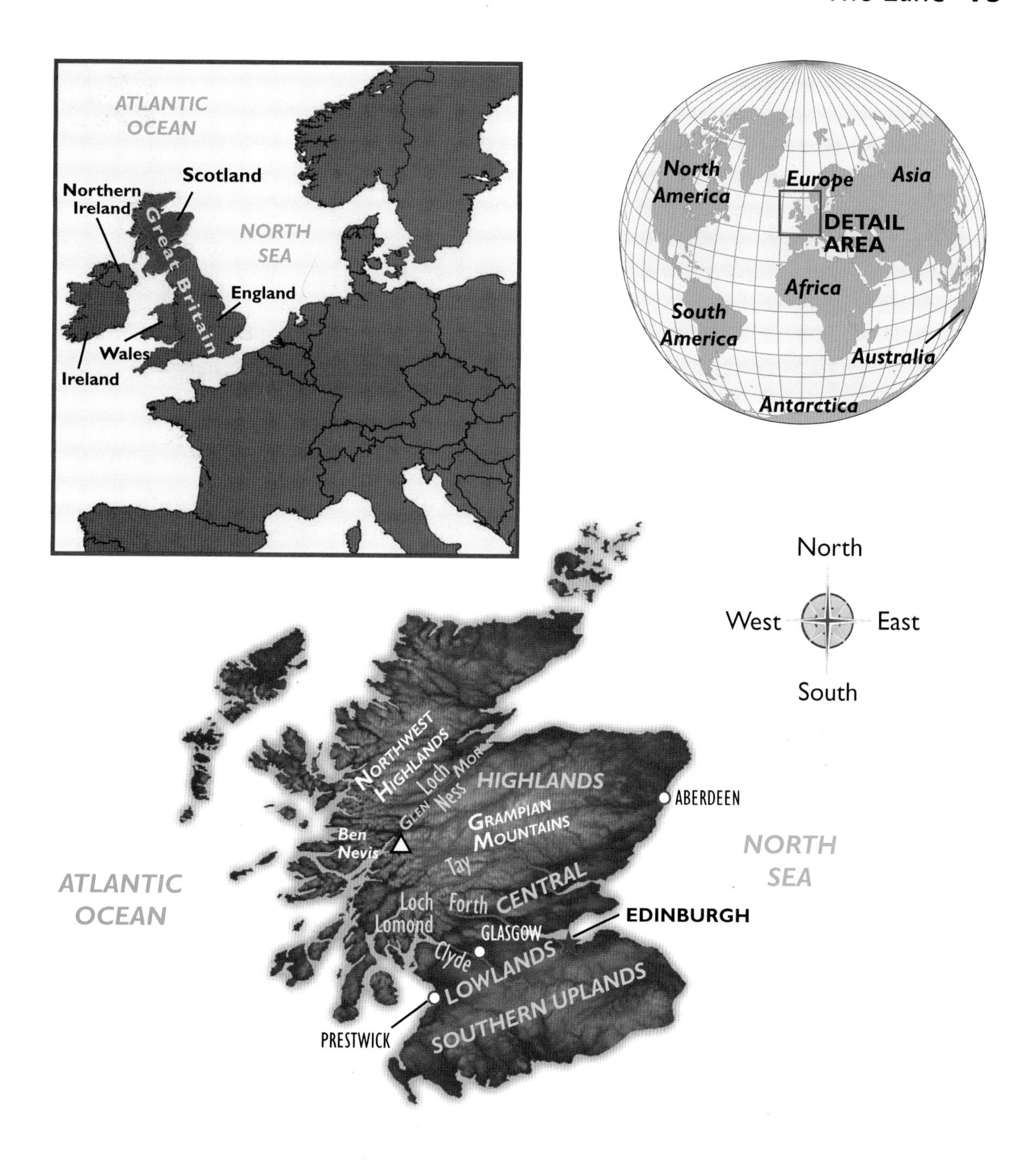
ATLANTIC OCEAN
Scotland
Northern Ireland
Great Britain
NORTH SEA
England
Wales
Ireland
North America
Europe
Asia
DETAIL AREA
Africa
South America
Australia
Antarctica
North
West
East
South
NORTHWEST HIGHLANDS
GLEN MOR
Loch Ness
HIGHLANDS
ABERDEEN
GRAMPIAN MOUNTAINS
Ben Nevis
Tay
NORTH SEA
ATLANTIC OCEAN
Loch Lomond
Forth
CENTRAL
EDINBURGH
GLASGOW
Clyde
LOWLANDS
PRESTWICK
SOUTHERN UPLANDS

South of the Highlands is the Central Lowlands. Here, rivers cross the land. They make the Lowlands a good area for farming. Most Scots live here. It is also where most of Scotland's major cities are located.

South of the Lowlands is the Southern Uplands. This area has **moors** with rocky cliffs. But parts of the Uplands have good pastures. They are excellent for raising livestock. The Uplands is also the border between Scotland and England.

Scotland's Ben Nevis, at 4,406 feet (1,343 m), is the highest mountain in the United Kingdom.

Rain

Rainfall

AVERAGE YEARLY RAINFALL

Inches		*Centimeters*
20 - 40		50 - 100
40 - 60		100 - 150
Over 60		Over 150

Temperature

AVERAGE TEMPERATURE

Fahrenheit		*Celsius*
Over 54°		Over 12°
43° - 54°	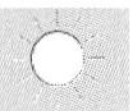	6° - 12°
32° - 43°		0° - 6°
21° - 32°		-6° - 0°

North

West East

South

Summer

Winter

Wild Things

Scotland is a small country with a variety of plants and animals. Much of Scotland has been cleared for agriculture. But in the Uplands, forests of Scotch pine, Norway spruce, and Douglas fir can be found.

The hills and mountains are covered by grasses and shrubs. Azalea, purple heather, and dwarf willow can also be found there. Peat moss grows in moist areas.

Purple heather

Scotland's forests are home to many different animals. Fox, badgers, red deer, wildcats, and pine marten are common. Red grouse and otters can also be found in Scotland.

Animals also live along Scotland's coasts. Porpoises and Grey seals are often seen playing near the shore. Whale watching is a common tourist activity in the summer. Sea birds such as gulls, gannets, and puffins nest on Scotland's shores.

Puffins are one type of sea bird that nest on Scotland's shores.

Scotland's people are trying to preserve their natural resources. There are 40 natural scenic areas where nature is protected by law.

The Scots

Scotland's people speak English and Scottish Gaelic. Many are Presbyterian. Most of Scotland's people live in the Lowlands. Many people in the cities live in row houses or apartment buildings. Today, many Scots own their own home.

Scots eat many delicious foods. They enjoy lamb and the famous Aberdeen-Angus (AH-bur-deen ANG-gus) beef. Since Scotland is surrounded by the sea, they also eat fish. Kippers and salmon are popular seafoods. Much cod is eaten in the form of fish and chips. This meal is fried fish fillets served with French fries.

Kippers are a common breakfast in Scotland.

A traditional food served on special occasions is haggis. It is made of the heart, liver, and lungs of a calf or sheep. These organs are mixed with onions, oats, and seasonings. The entire mixture is boiled in a pouch made from a sheep's stomach.

This butcher is holding haggis.

Scottish children between 5 and 16 must attend school. Almost all students wear uniforms. Secondary schools offer both **vocational** and **academic** courses. Scotland has 13 universities. The Universities of Edinburgh (EH-duhn-bur-uh) and Glasgow (GLAS-koh) are the largest.

Traditional Scottish clothing includes the kilt. It is a skirt-like garment. Most Scottish kilts are made from a clan's **tartan**. Tartans are often called plaids. Each clan's tartan is a different pattern and is used to identify clan members.

Traditional kilts are often worn by Highland farmers.

Skirlie

Skirlie is Scotland's national dish. It is good as stuffing for chicken, a side dish, or spread on toast.

- 2 ounces butter
- 1 onion, sliced
- 4 ounces finely cut oatmeal
- pinch of nutmeg, salt, and pepper for flavor

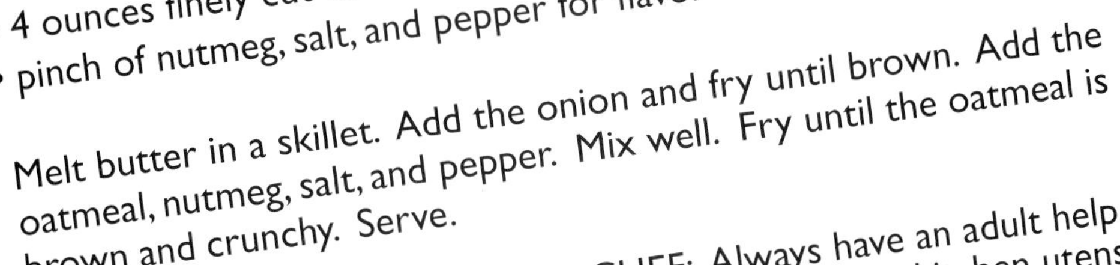

Melt butter in a skillet. Add the onion and fry until brown. Add the oatmeal, nutmeg, salt, and pepper. Mix well. Fry until the oatmeal is brown and crunchy. Serve.

AN IMPORTANT NOTE TO THE CHEF: Always have an adult help with the preparation and cooking of food. Never use kitchen utensils or appliances without adult permission and supervision.

English	Scottish Gaelic
Hello ________	Sodan (SODIHN)
Good-bye ________	Soraidh (SAWR-y)
Please ________	Toilich (TOLICH)
Thank you ________	Taing tu (TYNG too)
Mother ________	Mathair (MAY-hir)
Father ________	Daidein (DAY-dayn)

Making Money

Most of Scotland has poor soil. But farmers manage to grow potatoes, barley, oats, and wheat. Since growing crops is challenging, many farmers raise livestock.

Scotland is famous for its Aberdeen-Angus cattle. Scottish farmers also developed the Clydesdale horse and the Shetland pony. Scottish livestock farms produce meat, dairy products, and wool.

The sea surrounds Scotland. So many Scots earn their living by fishing. Haddock, cod, mackerel, herring, lobster, and prawn are important catches. The Scots catch almost all of the **United Kingdom's** fish and shellfish.

Some Scots earn a living by mining Scotland's natural resources. Coal is Scotland's chief mineral resource. Scotland's mines also produce gold, silver, and chromites.

Opposite page: There are six steps in brewing Scotch whisky. The fifth step is done in the stillroom of a distillery. Many stillrooms look similar to this one.

Scots manufacture automobiles, clocks and watches, **textiles**, and machinery. Scotland is also a center for printing and publishing. The *Encyclopædia Britannica* was first published there in 1768.

Brewing is another of Scotland's industries. Scots invented the famous Scotch whisky. It is one of Scotland's major exports each year.

Most Scots work in the service industry. They hold positions in retail, tourism, business, and transportation.

Important Places

Edinburgh is Scotland's capital. About 500,000 people live there. It is Scotland's center of medicine, law, banking, insurance, and tourism. Edinburgh's Port of Leith (LEETH) is Scotland's busiest port.

There are several learning institutions in Edinburgh. Scotland's National Library, the Scottish National Zoological park, and the Royal Scottish Museum are also there. The Chapel of St. Margaret is Edinburgh's oldest building. It was built around 1090.

Glasgow is Scotland's largest city. Glasgow is the commercial, industrial, and educational center of Scotland. It is located between the Highlands and the Lowlands. This makes it an important place for trade.

Glasgow has many things to see and do. The City Chambers and Glasgow Cathedral are located here. The Glasgow Art Gallery and Museum is an interesting place to visit. And the Glasgow ZooPark includes many of Scotland's native animals.

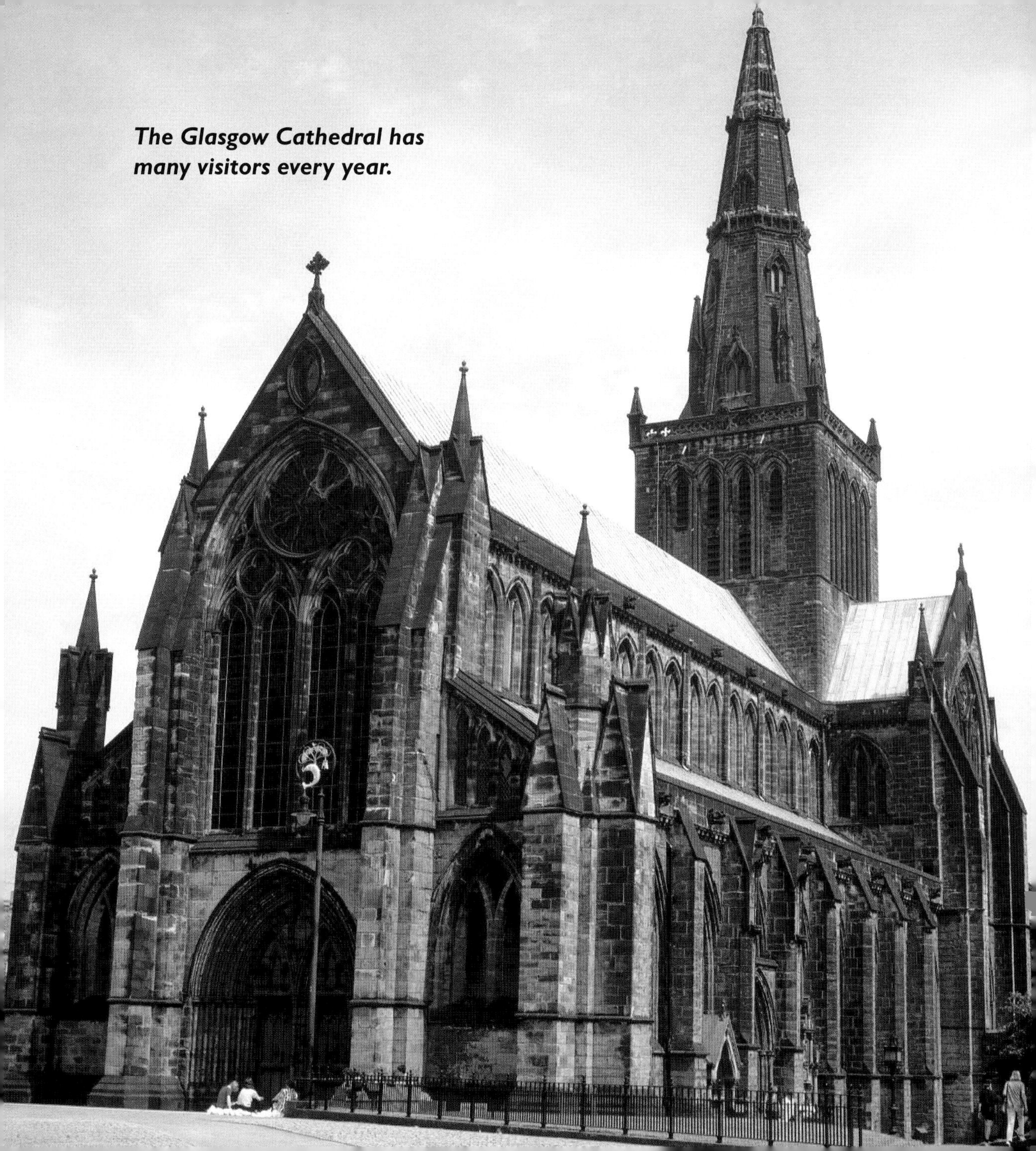

The Glasgow Cathedral has many visitors every year.

Getting Around

Most of Scotland is linked to the rest of Great Britain by highway. More than two million **vehicles** are registered in Scotland. So highways can get crowded.

Trains are another form of transportation in Scotland. Railroads serve major towns. Scotrail covers most of Scotland's cities. Britrail, the British railway system, also serves Scotland. Edinburgh's Waverly rail station is the second-largest station in the **United Kingdom**.

Scotland has major airports at Glasgow, Aberdeen, Prestwick (PREST-wik), and Edinburgh. The world's busiest **heliport** is located in Aberdeen. From there, people are taken by helicopter to and from the off-shore oil wells.

Ferries cross to the many islands of Scotland. They also bring people to mainland Europe.

Opposite page: Traveling by car in rural Scotland can be difficult. Sheep and other livestock can cause traffic jams!

The Government

Scotland is part of the **United Kingdom**, which is a **constitutional monarchy**. A king or queen is the head of state. A **prime minister** is the chief official. **Parliament** makes the laws.

Parliament is made up of the king or queen, the House of Commons, and the House of Lords. Members of the House of Lords inherit their seats. The people of the **United Kingdom** elect members of the House of Commons. It has 659 members. Scots elect 72 of them.

In 1979, Scots voted against having their own parliament. But in 1997, they passed a **referendum** to create a parliament of their own.

Scotland's parliament has 129 members. It governs Scotland's **domestic** affairs, such as education and housing. The British Parliament still controls foreign affairs, defense, and social security. Scotland's parliament met for the first time in 1999.

Opposite page: The Scottish Parliament's first meeting was in 1999.

Holidays & Festivals

Scotland's national holiday is St. Andrew's Night. St. Andrew is Scotland's patron saint. On November 30, Scots honor him. They celebrate with quiet dinners that include family and friends.

Many of Scotland's holidays are called bank holidays. This means Scotland's banks are closed, but other businesses may stay open. May Day is celebrated on the first day of May. Scots observe Spring Holiday on the last Monday in May. They celebrate Summer Holiday on the first Monday of August.

Scots observe religious holidays, too. Christmas is celebrated on December 25. The next day is called Boxing Day. On this day, Scots traditionally box up donations to give to the poor.

Hogmanay (hahg-muh-NAY) is the name of Scotland's New Year's celebration. Hogmanay is on January 1 and 2. But Scots begin celebrating the last week in December. They enjoy parades, street theaters, and fireworks. It is the biggest New Year's celebration in the world.

Fireworks during a Scottish celebration

Sports & Culture

Scots are credited with developing the modern game of golf. Scotland is home to one of the world's most famous courses. It is the Ancient Golf Club of St. Andrews.

Scots enjoy golf, but the most popular sport is soccer. In Scotland, the rules for soccer are the same as in the United States. But in Scotland, it is called football. Thirty-eight teams play in the Scottish Football League.

Many Scottish athletes participate each year in the Highland Games. Events include *cabar* tossing, racing, dancing, and bagpiping. A *cabar* (KAY-bur) is a tree trunk that is 20 feet (6 m) long and weighs 145 pounds (66 kg). Participants compete to see who can throw the *cabar* the farthest.

The cabar is so heavy it takes three men to bring it on the field! Scots have to be very strong to compete in this Highland game.

Scotland's beautiful landscape makes outdoor sports popular. In the Highlands, people hike, mountain climb, and shoot. In the winter, Scots enjoy skiing and playing a game called curling.

In curling, one player slides a heavy weight across the ice toward a goal. A teammate sweeps the ice in front of the sliding weight. This directs the weight toward the goal. The team whose weight is closest to the goal scores.

Bagpipes are an important part of Scottish **culture**. Bagpipers compete in the Highland Games. They also march in parades and play at festivals.

Literature is also part of Scottish culture. Many famous authors have come from Scotland. Sir Walter Scott was born in Edinburgh. He wrote the novel *Ivanhoe*. Robert Louis Stevenson was born in Edinburgh, too. He wrote *Kidnapped* and *Treasure Island.*

These men are participating in the Scottish Highland Games. Bagpiping is a test of breathing ability and musical talent!

Glossary

academic - relating to general education.
brewing - to prepare alcoholic drinks by steeping, boiling, and fermenting.
civil war - a war between groups in the same country.
constitutional monarchy - a form of government ruled by a king or queen who must follow the laws of a constitution.
covenant - a formal agreement.
culture - the customs, arts, and tools of a nation or people at a certain time.
domestic - of, relating to, or originating within a country.
economy - the way a nation uses its money, goods, and natural resources.
execute - to put to death according to law.
ferry - a boat used to carry people, goods, and cars across a body of water.
heliport - a place for helicopters to take off and land.
moor - an area of open, rolling, wild land, often covered with heather and having bogs and marshes.
parliament - the highest lawmaking body of some governments.
petroleum - a thick, yellowish-black oil. It is the source of gasoline.
prime minister - the highest-ranked member of some governments.
rebellion - an armed attack on a government.

referendum - a direct vote by the people on a public matter.
Reformation - a religious movement in the sixteenth century. People wanted to reform the Catholic Church. They formed Protestant churches by making these changes.
tartan - a plaid textile design of stripes of differing colors and sizes. Tartans are often used to identify clan members.
textiles - of or having to do with the designing, manufacturing, or producing of woven fabric.
United Kingdom - the united countries of England, Scotland, Wales, and Northern Ireland.
vehicle - a car, truck, or bus.
vocational - of or relating to training in a skill or trade to be pursued as a career.

Web Sites

Would you like to learn more about Scotland? Please visit **www.abdopub.com** to find up-to-date Web site links about Scotland's monarchs, mountains, and monsters. These links are routinely monitored and updated to provide the most current information available.

Index